American History & Government

Women in the Civil War

In Battle and at Home

by
Helen Sillett

Don Johnston Incorporated
Volo, Illinois

Edited by:

John Bergez
Start-to-Finish Core Content Series Editor, Pacifica, California

Gail Portnuff Venable, MS, CCC-SLP
Speech/Language Pathologist, San Francisco, California

Dorothy Tyack, MA
Learning Disabilities Specialist, San Francisco, California

Jerry Stemach, MS, CCC-SLP
Speech/Language Pathologist, Director of Content Development, Sonoma County, California

Graphics and Illustrations:

Photographs and illustrations are all created professionally and modified to provide the best possible support for the intended reader.

Front cover: Courtesy of Picture History
Page 7: Library of Congress, Prints and Photographs Division [LC-USZC2-1964]
Page 17: Library of Congress, Prints and Photographs Division [LC-ccph-3g04582]
Page 18: Library of Congress, Prints and Photographs Division [LC-DIG-cwpb-04322]
Page 20 and back cover: Library of Congress, Prints and Photographs Division [LC-USZ62-19319]
Page 22: Library of Congress, Prints and Photographs Division [LC-USZ62-93979]
Page 23 and back cover: Massachusetts Commandery Military Order of the Loyal Legion and the U.S. Army Military History Institute
Page 28: Virginia Historical Society
Page 30: Library of Congress, Prints and Photographs Division [LC-D4-33908]
Page 32: Library of Congress, Prints and Photographs Division [LC-DIG-cwpbh-01990]
Page 36: National Archives and Records Administration
Page 39: Library of Congress, Prints and Photographs Division [LC-USZ62-134453]
Page 44: Library of Congress, Prints and Photographs Division [LC-USZ62-7816]
Page 50: Library of Congress, Prints and Photographs Division [LC-DIG-cwpb-00821]
Page 51: Library of Congress, Prints and Photographs Division [LC-DIG-cwpb-01005]
Page 53: New York Public Library
Page 54: Library of Congress, Prints and Photographs Division [LC-USZ62-33264]
Page 55: Library of Congress, Prints and Photographs Division [LC-DIG-cwpb-04294]
Page 58: Abraham Lincoln Historical Digitization Project, Northern Illinois University Libraries
All other photos © Don Johnston Incorporated and its licensors.

Narration:

Professional actors and actresses read the text to build excitement and to model research-based elements of fluency: intonation, stress, prosody, phrase groupings and rate. The rate has been set to maximize comprehension for the reader.

Published by:

Don Johnston Incorporated
26799 West Commerce Drive
Volo, IL 60073

800.999.4660 USA Canada
800.889.5242 Technical Support
www.donjohnston.com

International Standard Book Number
ISBN-10: 1-4105-0676-2
ISBN-13: 978-1-4105-0676-4

Contents

The American Civil War

The Civil War split the United States into two parts: the North, which was also called the **Union**, and the South, which was also called the **Confederate states**.

The war began when 11 Southern states tried to leave the United States. These states wanted to become a new country because they thought that President Lincoln wanted to take away their right to own slaves. Lincoln fought to keep the United States together.

More than 600,000 Americans died in four years of fighting. In 1865, the North won the war and ended slavery in the United States.

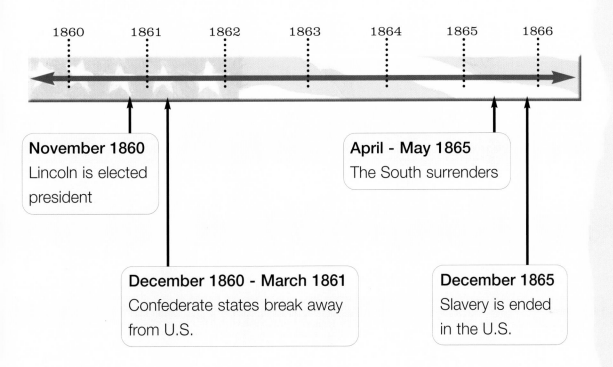

1860   1861   1862   1863   1864   1865   1866

November 1860
Lincoln is elected
president

December 1860 - March 1861
Confederate states break away
from U.S.

April - May 1865
The South surrenders

December 1865
Slavery is ended
in the U.S.

Getting Started

In 1864, a young soldier named Lyons Wakeman was fighting in a Civil War battle for the first time. It was a long and bloody day. For many hours, the Union and Confederate armies clashed on the battlefield. It was a nightmare. Cannons roared. Bullets flew through the air. Soldiers fell to the ground, screaming, as they were hit. Arms, legs, and even heads were torn off by cannonballs. The soldiers couldn't see where they were shooting because of all the smoke and dust in the air.

A Civil War battle

Lyons fought hard, just like the other soldiers on the battlefield that day. And just like the other soldiers, Lyons was glad to be alive when the day was over. But there was something different about this soldier. He had a secret — his real name was Sarah Rosetta Wakeman.

The other Union troops never guessed that the brave young soldier was actually a woman.

In those days, women weren't allowed to join the army. Sarah pretended to be a man so she could fight for the Union. Hundreds of other women in the North and the South did the same thing. Some women wanted the same chance as men to fight for their side. Some women fought to make money for their families. Other women wanted to have an adventure.

Women soldiers cared just as much about winning the war as men did. In 1862, a Northerner named Henry Clay Work wrote a song about women in the war. The song was called "We'll Go Down Ourselves."

In the song, women say they want to march on Richmond, Virginia, to help the Union win the war against the **rebels** (the Confederates). Richmond was the capital city of the South. Here are some of the words of the song:

> What shall we do, as years go by,
>
> And Peace remains a stranger —
>
> With Richmond yet in rebel hands,
>
> And Washington in danger? . . .
>
> What shall we do? What shall we do?
>
> Why, lay them on the shelves,
>
> And we'll go down ourselves,
>
> And teach the rebels something new,
>
> And teach the rebels something new.

Northern women didn't march on Richmond, but women on both sides did play a big part in the war. Women were soldiers, nurses, spies, and teachers. They made clothes for the troops. They made cases for bullets. At home, they worked in the fields and did other jobs while the men were away fighting.

These women made a big difference in the Civil War, but they did something more as well. They helped to teach Americans something new about what women could do.

Today, many people don't realize that some of the biggest heroes of the Civil War were women. In this book, you'll meet some of these women.

This Civil War picture shows women as heroes of the war.

Article 1

Women on the Battlefield

Questions this article will answer:

- **Why did Sarah Emma Edmonds join the Union army?**

- **Why didn't army leaders want women to work as nurses on the battlefield?**

- **How did Clara Barton help the Union side in the war?**

Would you risk being killed to fight for something you believed in?

During the Civil War, many women were ready to take that chance. "If only I were a man," Sarah Morgan wrote in her diary. She wanted to fight for the Confederate army.

Many women on both sides found a way to be a part of Civil War battles. Hundreds of women joined the fight by pretending to be men. Thousands more women worked as nurses. In this article, you'll read about some of the women who risked their lives on the battlefield during the war.

Women Soldiers

One of the most famous women soldiers in the Civil War was Sarah Emma Edmonds. Sarah dressed up as a man and joined the Union army as Franklin Thompson.

Sarah was born in Canada. After moving to the United States, she lived in the North. Sarah joined the army because she wanted to be a part of the fight. "I don't want to stay home and weep," she said.

Michigan Women's Hall of Fame

Sarah Emma Edmonds fought in the Union army during the Civil War.

As Franklin Thompson, Sarah worked as a nurse for her army unit. At the beginning of the war, most battlefield nurses were male soldiers. During battles, Sarah dodged bullets and cannonballs as she ran from one wounded man to the next. Many times, she could have been killed. The other soldiers in the unit said that she was not afraid of anything.

Other women from the North and the South pretended to be men so they could become soldiers. Some poor women joined the army to make money for their families. Some women signed up with their husbands or brothers.

When the war started, Elizabeth Niles and her husband, Martin, were on their honeymoon. Martin signed up right away to fight for the Union, and Elizabeth went with him.

Elizabeth cut her hair short, dressed as a man, and fought beside her husband. The army never found out that she was a woman.

The Need for Nurses

The Civil War was very bloody. About one out of every four soldiers either died or was hurt in the fighting. Many others died after getting hurt in accidents or becoming sick. In all, more than half a million soldiers lost their lives during the war. More than 400,000 other soldiers were wounded but survived.

More than 400,000 men were wounded
in Civil War battles.

Taking care of the wounded and dying
men was a huge job. Some women wanted
to help by becoming nurses, but at first the
armies didn't let them do it.

In those days, army doctors and their helpers were men. Army leaders said it wasn't right for women to work so closely with soldiers. They also thought that women shouldn't see the bloody side of the war. A battlefield hospital was a horrible sight. Often, doctors had to saw off injured arms and legs while soldiers screamed in pain. The arms and legs were tossed onto huge, bloody piles. Army leaders said that these field hospitals were no place for "ladies."

Hospitals on the battlefield were often just long rows of tents filled with wounded soldiers.

But women didn't want to stay away from the battlefield when there was so much useful work they could do. They didn't give up until they were allowed to care for men who were wounded in the war.

"The Angel of the Battlefield"

One of the most famous Civil War nurses was Clara Barton. Clara started out by bringing supplies to soldiers, but she wanted to do more. "While our soldiers stand and fight, I can stand and feed and nurse them," she said.

Clara Barton became a famous Civil War nurse.

Clara worked in the middle of many major battles. She followed the soldiers as they were fighting. She cooked food for the sick, and she put bandages on bloody wounds. She even used a small knife to dig bullets out of the flesh of wounded men.

Clara knew that she could die at any time. Sometimes her face was blue from smoke because she was so close to the guns being fired. Once, a bullet shot right through her dress. She was lucky that it didn't hit her body.

In one battle, Clara helped an army doctor who was operating on a wounded man. Bullets whizzed around their heads, but Clara didn't move until the job was done. Later, the doctor praised Clara in a letter. "She is a true heroine, the angel of the battlefield," he wrote.

Clara Barton was called the "angel of the battlefield."

Thousands of other women worked as nurses for the Union and Confederate armies. People soon noticed how brave they were. One grateful man said, "They worked like heroes night and day."

22

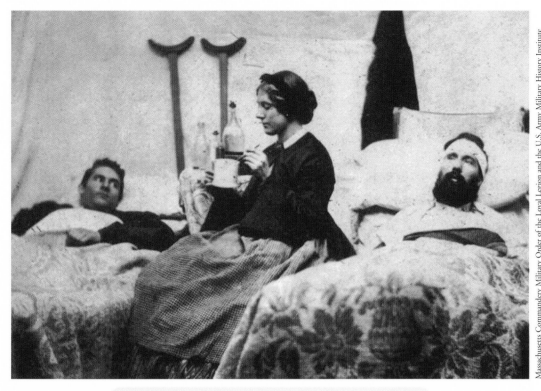

Wounded soldiers were grateful for the care they got from Civil War nurses.

Civil War nurses made people in the United States see that women could do many different jobs. Clara Barton is a good example. After the war, she was put in charge of the Missing Soldiers Office of the U.S. government. She was the first woman to lead an important government office.

Later, she was the first president of the American Red Cross. She and other Red Cross workers helped thousands of people after floods and other disasters.

Summary

In this article, you learned about women who helped on the battlefield during the Civil War. Some women pretended to be men so that they could join the army. Others talked army leaders into letting them work as nurses.

One of the most famous Civil War nurses was Clara Barton. She and thousands of other women risked their lives to care for wounded men. These Civil War nurses helped change ideas about the kinds of work that women in the United States could do.

Article 2

Spying on the Enemy

Questions this article will answer:

• **How did Elizabeth Van Lew help the Union?**

• **How did a teenage spy named Belle Boyd become famous?**

Imagine that you are a Southern woman during the Civil War. You find out that the Union army has cut off supplies to Confederate troops. You want to help the Southern soldiers. How could you bring guns and medicine to them without being found out?

Some Southern women found a clever answer to this question. They hid guns, clothes, and medicines under their long, full skirts. They also hid things in their umbrellas and even in their wigs.

Women in Civil War times often wore big, full skirts like the one in this picture.

Many of these women were caught,
but others didn't get stopped. Union soldiers
didn't think that charming ladies in long
silk dresses were really smuggling supplies
to Confederate troops.

Other women carried secret information.
These women were spies. They knew that
they could be put in jail, or even killed, if they
were caught.

Many women on both sides worked
as spies during the war. In this article,
you'll read about two of them.

"Crazy Bet," a Union Spy in the South

One of the Union's best spies was
a woman named Elizabeth Van Lew. Elizabeth
was from a rich family in the South, but she
risked her life to help the Union win the war.

Elizabeth was on the Union side because she hated slavery. She wanted slavery to be **abolished** (ended). Elizabeth spoke out against slavery in Richmond, Virginia, where she lived. She even used her money to buy slaves so she could set them free.

Elizabeth Van Lew worked as a spy for the Union because she hated slavery.

White people in Richmond thought that Elizabeth was crazy. They weren't used to hearing Southern women speaking against slavery. People started calling Elizabeth "Crazy Bet."

During the war, Elizabeth became a spy for the Union. She visited Union soldiers who were being held in Confederate prisons in Richmond. The men told her what they knew about the Confederate army, and Elizabeth sent the information to army leaders in the North. She didn't get caught, partly because people thought she was just a harmless crazy woman.

Elizabeth also set up a spy ring in Richmond. (A spy ring is a group of spies who work together secretly.) Some of Elizabeth's spies were African-American servants who had been her family's slaves.

The family had freed their slaves before the war, but many of them stayed on to work in Elizabeth's huge house. Elizabeth wrote letters in a secret code and the servants hid the letters in baskets of food and flowers. Then the servants traveled to Union army camps to pass along the information.

Elizabeth Van Lew lived in this house in Richmond, Virginia.

Elizabeth's spying was a success. Ulysses S. Grant, who was the Union's top general, said that Elizabeth and her spy ring helped him to fight the Confederate army. Today a sign at Elizabeth's grave says that she risked her life to end slavery and to keep the Union together.

Belle Boyd, a Teenage Spy

Another Southern woman, Belle Boyd, was still a teenager when she became famous as a spy for the Confederate side. Newspapers in both the North and the South wrote about her. Belle even married a Union officer — and got him to change sides and support the South!

Belle was 17 when Union soldiers took over her town in Virginia. She was a charming young woman, and she used her charm to begin spying for the South.

Belle flirted with Union soldiers and tried to find out their plans. One time, she learned some secrets that she wanted to pass on to Stonewall Jackson, who was a Confederate general. Belle rode through the night on horseback to bring the information to Jackson's camp. She had to talk the Union guards into letting her reach the camp.

Belle Boyd was a spy for the Confederates.

Belle was arrested for spying several times. She became so well-known as a Confederate spy that she couldn't fool people any more, so she began carrying messages for the Confederates instead.

In 1864, Belle traveled to England with some Confederate letters. In England, she married a Union officer who had fallen in love with her and followed her there. When Belle's husband went back to the United States, he began working for the South.

Belle may have liked being famous as much as she liked being a spy. In England, she became an actress. After the war, she was in plays in the United States. She also dressed up in a Confederate uniform and gave talks about her Civil War adventures.

Summary

In this article, you learned about two women who worked as spies during the Civil War. Elizabeth Van Lew lived in the South, but she wanted to help the Union because she hated slavery. She set up a spy ring to pass information to Union leaders. Belle Boyd became a famous Confederate spy when she was still a teenager. After the war, she gave talks about her life as a spy in the Civil War.

Article 3

Working at Home and Helping the Troops

Questions this article will answer:

• **Why did women take on new jobs during the Civil War?**

• **How did women support the troops?**

• **Who helped sign up African Americans for the Union army?**

During the Civil War, some women traveled far and wide as soldiers, nurses, or spies.

35

Many other women did their part by staying close to home. These women might not have had as many adventures as spies or soldiers, but they did a lot of important work during the war. This article tells you what they did.

Filling in for Men

About three million men left their jobs and families to fight in the Civil War. Someone had to do their work while they were gone. Often, women took over these jobs.

Some women took jobs in factories and mills. They worked to make shoes and clothes. Other women took over office jobs that had been held by men. Sadly, women were paid much less money than men for the same jobs.

Many families became poor during the Civil War because women were not paid well for their work.

Women did many new kinds of work during the Civil War. This woman, Mary Tippee, drove wagons loaded with food and other things that she sold to Union soldiers.

Other women helped to run their family farms. One woman said, "Our worker left to fight just as corn planting began, so I put my hoe on my shoulder and went out into the fields, and I have worked there ever since. I guess my work is just as good as his."

People noticed all the women working hard on their family farms. "I met more women than men on the road, driving teams of animals. And I saw more women than men at work in the fields," one traveler said.

Supporting the Troops

As soon as the war started, thousands of women in the North and the South began working to support the troops. Rich women, poor women, black women, and white women — all of them did their part. Some women worked in groups making cases for bullets.

Poor farm women made yarn that would be used to knit clothes for the soldiers. Rich women bought uniforms for whole **regiments**. (A regiment is a large group of soldiers in an army. One Civil War regiment could have a thousand soldiers in it.)

This Civil War newspaper showed a picture of women helping to make cases for bullets.

Many women sewed uniforms for the soldiers. Some women worked alone in their houses. Other women started sewing groups. Some women even set up sewing factories.

Knitting was another way that women helped the soldiers. Women knitted socks and gloves to send to the troops. Some women knitted when they got together with their friends. Other women knitted as they rode in carriages that were pulled by horses. If you walked around a city in the North or the South, you would even have seen women knitting as they walked along the street.

In Charleston, South Carolina, women made so many socks that one Confederate soldier complained about it. He said that he had dozens of socks and just one shirt. He wished they would make him more shirts and not so many socks!

Women helped in other ways as well. In the South, women raised money for building gunboats and buying other supplies. When battles took place near their homes, women on both sides took the troops into their homes and cooked for them. They also cared for soldiers who were wounded.

Working so close to the fighting could be dangerous. Jennie Wade was shot and killed while she was making bread for Union troops at the battle of Gettysburg. When she was buried, she still had bread dough on her hands and arms.

Jennie Wade was the only woman who was killed in the battle of Gettysburg.

Signing Up Black Troops

Women also helped by getting men to join the fight. Some famous African-American women signed up black men to fight for the Union army. This was an important job because the Union needed more men.

One of these women was Harriet Tubman. You may have heard of her. She is famous for helping slaves to escape from the South. But Harriet also did many other important things during her life. One of them was traveling to the South to look for former slaves. (Former slaves were people who had been slaves but now were free). She asked these men to fight for the Union army.

In 1863, Harriet Tubman led 750 former slaves out of the South to join the Union side.

Harriet Tubman helped sign up black soldiers to fight in the Union army.

Mary Ann Shadd Cary was another African-American woman who got black troops to sign up. Mary Ann was well educated, and she was a famous **abolitionist** (someone who wanted slavery to end). She was also the first African-American woman to run a weekly newspaper.

Mary Ann Shadd Cary was the first African-American woman to run a weekly newspaper.

45

In 1864, Mary Ann became a **recruiter** for the Union army. This means that she had the job of getting men to sign up. Mary Ann gave speeches and wrote articles about the fight to end slavery in the South. She traveled around giving talks to get black men to fight for the Union.

Summary

In this article, you learned how women were able to help out during the Civil War even when they didn't leave home. Many women took new jobs to take over for men who were away fighting. Others worked to support the troops. Women made bullet cases and clothes for the soldiers.

When the fighting came near their homes, they nursed wounded men, and they gave the troops food and places to stay. Harriet Tubman and Mary Ann Shadd Cary helped to get black men to sign up for the Union army.

Article 4

Helping Former Slaves

Questions this article will answer:

- **Why did Charlotte Forten travel to the South during the Civil War?**

- **Frances Beecher helped teach some men to read and write. Who were these men?**

- **How did women in the North help runaway slaves and freed slaves?**

Soon after the beginning of the Civil War, groups of slaves began arriving at Union army camps. The slaves had run away from their owners. The war had given them the chance to get what they had always wanted — their freedom.

A Northern woman named Laura Hildreth saw some of these **runaway slaves** at one camp. The runaway slaves "come in every day," she wrote to her sister. "It was a sad sight to see the poor creatures, homeless, not knowing when or where they were going to get their next meal."

The men in this photo ran away from their owners and escaped to a Union army camp.

As the war went on, more and more slaves escaped or were set free by Union armies. Women played a big role in helping the former slaves start new lives as free people. In this article, you'll meet some of the women who helped them.

Teaching Former Slaves

When the war began, most of the slaves in the South didn't know how to read or write.

It was against the law to teach slaves. Slave owners thought that it was easier to keep their slaves in line if the slaves had not learned to read or write.

When slaves became free, learning to read and write was one of the first things that many of them hoped for. They knew that this would give them a better life.

These former slaves escaped to freedom during the Civil War. They needed schools so they could learn to read and write.

Many Northern women traveled to the South to set up schools for former slaves. One of these women was a young African-American teacher named Charlotte Forten. Charlotte left her home in the North and traveled to some islands off the coast of South Carolina. The Union army had taken over these islands, and they had freed all the slaves there. Charlotte wanted to teach these men, women, and children to read and write.

Charlotte Forten traveled to the South
to teach freed slaves.

Later, Charlotte wrote about what it was
like to teach freed slaves. "I never before
saw children so eager to learn," she wrote.
The adults wanted to learn, too. "One old
woman came to school and took her seat
among the little ones," Charlotte remembered.
"She was at least sixty years old."

Another woman came to class carrying her baby in her arms.

Northern women, both black and white, helped to teach former slaves in the South. After the war was over, African Americans began setting up their own schools to teach the children of former slaves.

Many Northern women taught in schools for former slaves.

Teaching Black Soldiers

During the war, the Union army began forming regiments of black soldiers. Some of these men were freed slaves from the South. Others were runaways. Women worked in the army camps, teaching these former slaves how to read and write.

Many black soldiers in the Union army were former slaves. The wives of army leaders helped teach some of these men to read and write.

55

One of these women was Frances Beecher. Frances was the wife of a Union army officer. She helped to teach the black men in her husband's regiment.

Frances wrote that she set up her school "wherever our moving tents were pitched." She was very proud of her work. When the men first joined the regiment, they didn't even know how to write their own names. They had to sign for their pay with an X or other mark. Before long, they were able to sign their names to get their pay.

The soldiers were excited about learning, even when they weren't in class. "Whenever they had a spare moment, out would come a spelling book," Frances said. "And you would often see a group of heads around one book."

Helping Former Slaves
Start a New Life

Many Northern women found other ways of helping former slaves. One of these women, Elizabeth Keckley, had once been a slave herself. During the war, she worked as a dressmaker for President Lincoln's wife, Mary Todd Lincoln. Elizabeth wanted to help slaves who had escaped from the South and moved to Washington. She decided to start a group to raise money for them.

As Mrs. Lincoln's dressmaker, Elizabeth met many rich and powerful people. She never missed a chance to ask people to give money for her group. To raise more money, she set up branches of her group in other cities. She even asked friends in England to give money to help former slaves start new lives.

Elizabeth Keckley raised money to help former slaves start their new lives.

Other women helped in any way they could. Lydia Maria Child saved $200 by not buying as much butter, sugar, or clothes. She gave the money to a group that was helping former slaves. Martha Wright gave almost all her family's clothes to former slaves.

You have already read how Northern women sewed uniforms for Union soldiers. Some of these women began sewing clothes for former slaves instead. Women's groups also sent supplies to hospitals for former slaves.

Summary

In this article, you learned how women helped slaves who escaped to freedom during the Civil War. Some women traveled to the South to teach reading and writing. Women also taught former slaves in the Union army. Other women, like Elizabeth Keckley, raised money. Women in the North also sewed clothes and sent supplies to hospitals for former slaves. All these women — like the others you have read about in this book — played an important part in the Civil War.

Glossary

Word	Definition	Page
abolish	to end	28
abolitionist	someone who wanted slavery to be **abolished** (ended)	45
Confederate states	The Confederate states were the Southern states in the Civil War. The Southern soldiers were called Confederates.	4
rebels	people who fight against their own government	9
recruiter	a person who gets others to join an organization, such as the army	46
regiment	a large group of soldiers in an army	39
runaway slaves	slaves who had run away from their owners	49
Union	The Union was the Northern states in the Civil War.	4

About the Author

Helen Sillett was born in England and lived in the Netherlands and Canada before moving to California as a teenager. She has taught history and literature classes to college students, and reading and writing classes to young adults. She is a writer and editor and has been a member of the Start-to-Finish team for several years.

Helen lives with her husband and their dog, Ella, in Los Angeles.

About the Narrator

Barbara Figgins graduated from Northwestern University with a degree in Theatre and has worked at many theaters across the country. She has also worked in film, television and radio. Being a part of this project has been great fun and educational as well! It is always nice to learn something new.

A Note to the Teacher

Start-to-Finish Core Content books are designed to help students achieve success in reading to learn. From the provocative cover question to the carefully structured and considerate text, these books promote inquiry, active engagement, and understanding. Not only do students learn curriculum-relevant content, but they learn how to read with understanding. Here are some of the features that make these books such powerful aids in teaching and learning.

Structure That Supports Inquiry and Understanding

Core Content books are carefully structured to encourage students to ask questions, identify main ideas, and understand how ideas relate to one another. The structural features of the Gold Core Content books include the following:

- **"Getting Started"**: A concise introduction engages students in the book's topic and explicitly states what they will learn.
- **Clearly focused articles:** Each of the following articles focuses on a single topic at a length that makes for a comfortable session of reading.
- **"Questions This Article Will Answer"**: Provocative questions following the article title reflect the article's main ideas. Each question corresponds to a heading within the article.
- **Article introduction:** An engaging opening leads to a clear statement of the article topic.
- **Carefully worded headings:** The headings within each article are carefully worded to signal the main idea of the section and reflect the opening questions.
- **Clear topic statements:** Within each article section, the main idea is explicitly stated so that students can distinguish it from supporting details.
- **"Summary"**: A brief Summary in each article recaptures the main ideas signaled by the opening questions, text headings, and topic statements.

Text That Is Written for Success™

Every page of a Core Content book is the product of a skilled team of educators, writers, and editors who understand your students' needs. The text features of these books include the following:

- **Mature treatment of grade level curriculum:** Core Content is age and grade-appropriate for the older student who is actively acquiring reading skills. The books also contain information that may be new to any student in the class, empowering Core Content readers to contribute interesting information to class discussions.
- **Idioms and vocabulary:** The text limits the density of new vocabulary and carefully introduces new words, new meanings of familiar words, and idioms. New subject-specific terms are bold-faced and included in the Glossary.
- **Background knowledge:** The text assumes little prior knowledge and anchors the reader using familiar examples and analogies.
- **Sentence structure:** The text uses simple sentence structures whenever possible, but where complex sentences are needed to clarify links between ideas, the structures used are those which research has shown to enhance comprehension.

For More Information

To find out more about Start-to-Finish Core Content, visit www.donjohnston.com for full product information, standards and research base.